The Missing Snake

by Maryann Dobeck
illustrated by Lisa Blackshear

Scott Foresman

Editorial Offices: Glenview, Illinois • New York, New York
Sales Offices: Reading, Massachusetts • Duluth, Georgia
Glenview, Illinois • Carrollton, Texas • Menlo Park, California

My name is Jane.
Is something missing? Call me. I can take the case.

I find missing planes.
I find missing canes. I
find missing skates.

Dave came to see me.
"Jake is missing," said Dave.
"Jake is my pet snake."

Dave looked for Jake. He looked in his cage. He looked in the tub.

Dave called Jake. He yelled his name.

"You make me laugh," I said. "A snake can not call back."

"Come with me," I said.
"I will go after Jake. I will find him for you."

We looked and looked.
We looked by the bed. We
looked by the games.

We looked some more. We looked by the vase. We looked by the gate.

"It is late," said Dave.
"It is time for bed."
"That's it!" I yelled.

"I know where Jake is!"
I said. "Jake likes to sleep.
I bet he is in bed!"

Dave laughed. He said, "You are good. You cracked the case!"

Phonics for Families: This book features words with long *a*, as in *snake* and *Jane*, as well as words ending with the letters *-ed*, as in *looked* and *yelled*. It also provides practice reading the high-frequency words *call*, *after*, *laugh*, and *something*. Read the book together. Then have your child name words that rhyme with *snake*.

Phonics Skills: Long *a* (CVCe); Inflected ending *-ed* (without spelling change)

High-Frequency Words: *call, after, laugh, something*